UFOs

The Most Compelling Evidence
for The Existence of UFOs

Copyright 2017 by From Hero To Zero - All rights reserved.

TABLE OF CONTENTS

ABOUT THE BOOK

Unidentified Flying Objects, like religion, have found a way to divide humanity; one-third into believers, another third into sceptics, and the remaining third not really knowing where they stand. The search for answers, like religion, has also been constant dead ends. Now we cannot deny the fact that once in a while strange things happen in our skies. However, people seem to make the assumption that an unidentified flying object is directly correlated to alien life. Fact? No. A UFO simply refers to anything in flight that cannot be identified or explained through conventional reasoning. This being said, it would not be irrational to relate the two, but the initial is not always as a result of the former.

In this book, we shall cover in about twenty chapters the most infamous UFO sightings, encounters, and even abductions of all time. Some of the accounts leave behind an eerie, chilly feeling as one goes through them with the thought that we might not be the only ones in the universe, but some, as is very common, are merely publicity stunts or are as a result of sycophancy.

It is worth noting also that one cannot really pinpoint the first ever UFO sighting. Human beings have had a knack for being curious for quite a while now. From as far back as before Christ, people reported seeing strange objects in the sky. However, life back then was much simpler, and people always assumed that all of these strange objects were a result of religious interventions.

We certainly hope that this book will go a long way into breaking down the world's most infamous UFO sightings and accounts of Interstellar coming together. There are too many UFO sightings to fit in one e-book, but we also have attempted to make this book as factual as it could be. However, this is not to say that every account in here is true. Most UFO sightings are marred with inconsistent tales, and we have tried to sum up, through research, what we believe were the actual events. Also, we hope that you are able to distinguish between the writer's opinion and facts.

Do enjoy your read and feel free to venture through the internet in search of other books on the same subject as we cannot possibly exhaust everything on unidentified flying objects.

INTRODUCTION

Unidentified Flying Objects, better known as UFOs, can refer to any object in the sky that can neither be identified as planes and rockets or astrological phenomena, such as comets or meteors. Despite the fact that most of these objects are later on identified, some of them never are. This may be a result of the lack of a straight explanation or lack of sufficient evidence. This leads to the assumption that these unidentified flying objects are caused by an intervention of extraterrestrial life. The term itself, UFO, came into being in 1953 and was coined by the Air Force of the United States of America as a general term for all such reports and incidents. A UFO was initially classified as any object that was airborne which did not resemble anything else in functionality, appearance, or even aerodynamics.

UFO sightings go back as far as possibly 467 BC. However, it is safe to assume that most of the occurrences back then were astrological phenomena since there was no real way to determine which was which. However, sightings were not attributed to extraterrestrials, but were rather seen as mainly religious signs. The first ever 'legitimate' UFO sighting claim in recent history was in 1978 on the 25th of January. A farmer claimed that he saw circular objects that were both large and dark flying at a great speed. In this book, we shall attempt to break down some of the most infamous sightings of the 20th and 21st centuries. The 20th, however, was the most notorious for UFO sightings.

CHAPTER ONE: KENNETH ARNOLD CASE, 1947

Kenneth Arnold case was the first of the post-World War II era, which saw quite a substantial number of UFO sighting claims. Mr. Arnold, a private pilot, asserted in 1947 on the 24th of June that he saw objects that he couldn't identify. He stated that there were nine in number and very shiny. The location of the sighting was North of Mount Rainier.

The pilot, while flying to Yakima, Washington heard of a handsome reward for anyone who would discover a crashed airplane that belonged to the US Marines and was used to transport them, and so took a diversion. However, after a few minutes of fruitless searching, he gave up and decided to continue with his journey to Yakima. A short while later, he claims to have seen flashing lights that were very bright and then subsequent flashes a couple of seconds after the first. His initial thought was that he was very near to another airplane. He ran some tests on his radar but could not locate any plane in the vicinity, thus ruling out that possibility. The bright flashes then flew past him at breakneck speed, which he estimated to be at about 12000 mph (1,932 kph). His second assumption was that these were birds, geese for an instant, but that did not seem plausible for a number of obvious reasons such as the speed they were moving at, the altitude, and the flashing lights.

The objects were moving towards Mount Rainier. He described the flying objects as convex shaped, which spun erratically and were grouped together. He compared them to discs or saucers skipping on water. They then flew behind the mountain and disappeared. He steered his aircraft southward, opened his window and started observing them without any distractions.

Through the equipment on his plane and his knowledge, he calculated their flight speed. The nine objects flew an estimate of 50 miles in just under two minutes, 82 seconds to be precise, which would mean they flew in excess of 1,700 mph (2700 kph). This meant that these strange objects arguably flew at thrice the speed of any precedence set by any type of aircraft in man's control by the year 1947. Keep in mind also that back then the sound barrier had not been broken, but the flying disks did so.

Arnold soon landed in Yakima where he was headed to in the first place at around 1600hrs. He immediately told his story to the staff and his friends at the airport. The story spread and caught on like wildfire. This, however, would bring a lot of publicity into his life, which he complained about. He claimed that his life had been restless ever since the incident with people constantly nagging him. He was even quoted saying that a certain preacher called him to say that those were signs of the end; "doomsday" he'd said. People labelled him anything from Einstein to a lunatic depending on whether they believed his story or not.

In light of the negativity, however, most of the responses he got were rather positive with many people writing to him seeking to work together in order to solve this mystery. This put a really strong emphasis on the subject of the possibility of life outside of earth. However, it being 1947, a lot of focus was placed on religious interventions. The pilot, Kenneth Arnold resolved to buy a camera which he would take with him everywhere during his flight hours in the hopes of capturing any other sightings.

A man by the name of Fred Johnson vouched for Arnold's sightings, reporting on the same day he had also seen objects, six of them, that were not dissimilar to Mr. Arnold's through his telescope. The main corroboration came in on July 4th, Independence Day, 10 days after Kenneth Arnold's sighting. A crew of a United Airlines flight was flying to Seattle over Idaho when they made sightings of objects that flew past their plane then disappeared. There were five to nine objects and they were shaped like disks. The pilot of the plane, Captain Emil J. Smith, the co-pilot, and Kenneth Arnold met the following day to compare notes. Similarities were in plenty and Arnold felt that the sightings of the two pilots were credible. The two, Arnold and Smith eventually became friends.

Arnold's sighting is widely credited with coining the term *"flying saucers"* as we know them today, since that it was how it was described in newspapers that ran the story the following couple of days. Subsequently, June 24th is celebrated as World UFO Day as a result of Kenneth Arnold's account of a UFO encounter.

The following month, the most infamous UFO sighting of them all happened, ***July 8th, 1947, Roswell.***

CHAPTER TWO: ROSWELL, 1947

Barely a month after the Kenneth Arnold sighting, the most famous, most reported, and most investigated UFO incident happened in Roswell, on July 8th, 1947. On a ranch near Roswell in New Mexico, an unidentified flying object crashed. The United States military was quick to step in and claim that it was simply a weather balloon that had crashed on the ranch. There are photos suggesting that it was a weather balloon. However, the suspicious nature of Roswell's handling led sceptics to believe that there was a lot more that the public did not know. All the way into the seventies, there was very minimal talk and general interest in the case. However, in 1970, a whole generation later, conspiracy theories by famed ufo-ologists emerged. They claimed that the military had seized both a crashed spacecraft and the extraterrestrial beings that occupied it.

Here is the full account.

In the summer of 1947, on July the 8th, an unidentified flying object crashed on a ranch in Roswell. The military swooped in and claimed that this was simply a conventional weather balloon; **Project Mogul.** They held onto this story, but amidst growing speculation and suspicion, they altered their statement and said that the crash was a result of a nuclear testing. Their story worked, and interest in Roswell died down for thirty years.

However, 3 weeks earlier on June the 14th, a foreman, about 30 miles from the actual crash site had discovered some debris on his farm. The debris, which had matched the report, consisted of strips of rubber, sticks, foils of tin, and paper. He collected most of it and stored it. On July 4th, the foreman, William Brazel, heard reports of a flying disk that had crashed in

Roswell and decided to see the Sheriff about it. Reports led to suggest that in private discussions with the Sheriff, Mr. Brazel had stumbled upon that he considered to be a flying saucer. After investigations and analysis, it was established that the debris that Mr. Brazel had collected were also from the same balloon. This convinced the public because it could be proven beyond reasonable doubt that there was nothing out of the ordinary with the crash.

Amidst a swarm of conspiracy theories, the Roswell incident sprung back up between 1978 and 1990, 30 years after it happened. UFO researchers over the years questioned hundreds of people in and around Rowell, including supposed witnesses and those who were directly involved with the handling of the case, and some few things did not hold up. They also acquired documents and reports, some of which were claimed to be leaked by insiders. They inferred that there was the possibility of not just a spacecraft that had crashed, but that there were alien bodies too. They insisted that the government had been quick to gather it all and perhaps pull the biggest cover up ever.

To add onto this, the only person that had accompanied the debris from the crash scene to Fort Worth where it was kept and studied, Jesse Marcel was interviewed in 1978 by author Stanton Friedman, and he gave a different account. He claimed that the government's reports were untrue and that they were hiding something. This further fuelled the Roswell conspiracy fires.

Books, TV series, and articles began to pop up everywhere further causing the public to believe not only in the crash of an unusual spacecraft but also in extraterrestrial life.

Renowned sceptics Joe Nickell and co-creator James McGaha recognized a myth-production process, which they called the "Roswellian Syndrome" In this disorder, a myth is suggested to comprise of five particular phases of advancement: **Incident,**

Debunking, Submergence, Mythologizing, and Re-emergence and Media Bandwagon Effect. The creators anticipated that the Roswellian Syndrome was highly likely to occur again in other UFO and paranoid idea stories.

It is, however, worth noting that leading up to its widespread publicity, there were conflicting accounts by both witnesses and ufo-ologists. The accounts vary and even contradict each other across the board, not to mention the lack of any concrete evidence by the researchers. In conclusion, whether true or not, the American Military and government were and still are the biggest winners of the incident or Roswell. They managed to produce stellar evidence that there was nothing peculiar with the Roswell crash, leaving believers and ufo-ologists scampering to prove their case.

CHAPTER THREE: WASHINGTON, DC
1952 *(Project Blue Book)*

The sightings in Washington DC were a series of events rather than just a single sighting. A variety of names were given to it, for instance **, Washington Flap** and **The Washington Invasion.** The sightings of Unidentified Flying Objects took place in the summer of 1953 between the 12th and 29th of July. Coincidentally, the most heavily reported sightings came in on consecutive weekends, on the 19th-20th and 26th-27th.

Edward Nugent was working as an air traffic controller at what was then the Washington National Airport, which was later renamed after the 40th American president, Ronald Reagan. Nugent was working on July 19[th,] which was Saturday at about twenty minutes to noon. On his radar appeared seven objects which were 15 miles southwest of the city. The objects were strange for two reasons, they did not follow any designated flight paths, and at the time no aircraft were supposed to be in that airspace. The air traffic controller informed his superior, Harry Barnes, who took time to observe the object on Nugent radar. He immediately concurred that they were strange as they did not adhere to typical aircraft movements and motions.

After speculation that Edward Nugent's equipment was faulty, Mr. Barnes had it checked, but it was working well. Harry Barnes made a number of calls and the National Airport's control tower also established that their radars, just like Nugent's, had also picked up strange 'blips.' They also told Mr. Barnes that a bright light zoomed past them at immense speed in the sky.

It was then that on all radars in the airport objects appeared. Not only in the airport, but all over Washington they popped up, with several army bases and pilots reporting such similar sightings.

These happenings were heavily published and they made the front pages of almost every other newspaper, but this was just one-half of the sightings.

Similarly, the following weekend, July 26th, in the early morning at around 8 AM, a pilot and a steward working on a National Airline airplane flying to the capital, Washington DC, saw some bizarre lights from above their plane. Radars at both the **Andrews Air Force Base** and the **National Airport** began picking up unknown objects just a few minutes later. About 80 minutes later unknown objects were being detected in all sectors of the radar's range.

Two jets were summoned and flew over the areas where the blips were located. One jet was manned by flight leader, Captain John McHugo. He, however, after recurrent attempts, found and saw nothing! William Patterson, a Lieutenant, and Captain McHugo's wingman, saw four white glows. At top speed, he tried to chase them, but soon gave up because they were moving much faster than he was. When he was asked whether he saw anything, he replied that they were all around him and he asked base what he should do but did not get any answer since nobody had the slightest clue what they were.

Radar and weather specialists were deployed, but other than negligible weather anomaly (a temperature inversion) there was nothing concrete to explain and sum up the odd occurrences. Civilian planes flying into Washington on the same day also reported bizarre flashing things. However, the sightings completely disappeared and ended the following morning.

As is expected, and just like the first sightings merely the previous weekend, this story made headlines! The public became anxious. In a bid to calm the general public, the Air Force summoned the press to explain the happenings at the

Pentagon. This happened to be the largest press conference, only second to that following World War II, to be held by the Pentagon. The key speakers, who were deemed experts in matters regarding UFOs from the Air Force, included Generals John Samford and Roger Ramey.

General Samford explained that the UFOs were nothing but astrological phenomena that were simply misunderstood, such as meteors and stars. He went on to say that the objects were not of any solid nature and could not have been material and/or tangible. The occurrences were blamed on the temperature inversion that had been witnessed on that day.

Despite the Air Force's best efforts to explain it, doubts crept in. Not only did the temperature inversion theory not provide any stellar proof, but these inversions were very common in the summer. Likewise, the inversion will appear on radars as a straight line rather than a blip or an object. Another explanation that disproved General Samford's theory is that some people actually got to see the physical objects, which went contrary to what he purported that they were not.

A panel called **Project Blue Book** was set up to try and demystify the occurrences of the summer of '52 in Washington, but to this date, their biggest breakthrough has been in silencing not only the Washington Flap, but any other UFO cases rather than solving of them.

CHAPTER FOUR: SHAG HARBOR, 1967

A UFO incident was reported in Shag Harbor. This was located in Nova Scotia, Canada, known to be inhabited by simple fishermen in the year 1947 on the night of October 4th. Locals of the village, at least eleven people, claimed they saw an object that was very low and flying towards Shag Harbour. They heard something like a whistling sound followed by a crash. The incident was first reported by a resident, Laurie Wickens and four of his friends. Wickens then contacted the **Royal Canadian Mounted Police (RCMP).**

The RCMP proceeded to contact a rescue center (RCC) making the assumption that an aircraft had crashed and so were concerned for survivors. However, after about half an hour of searching by both the RCC and local fishermen and their boats, no survivors, bodies, nor debris were found. By morning, the RCC had established that no aircraft had crashed since none was missing. Underwater, searches were conducted just for clarity's sake, but still, nothing was found.

CHAPTER FIVE: THE HILL ABDUCTION, 1961

September 19th and 20th are the dates Barney and Betty Hill of New Hampshire claim they were abducted by extraterrestrial beings. The incident was also later called the 'Zeta Reticuli incident' because the couple claimed that the aliens were from the Zeta Reticuli system.

The couple was driving back home from a vacation in Montreal and Niagara Falls. Betty thought she saw a falling star that was moving below the moon. However, the falling star was growing brighter and bigger and was moving in an erratic motion. She urged her spouse to stop the car so that they could observe it better. Betty grabbed a pair of binoculars and saw a craft that looked bizarre and had flashing lights that were multi-colored. She immediately thought that it had to be a flying saucer as her sister had confided to her of a UFO sighting a few years back. Barney, however, held that it was just a regular airplane. In a matter of moments, the supposed airplane sharply began to drop in his direction, which led him to believe that he had judged it wrongly. They got back into their vehicle and drove on to perhaps get a better view.

After about a mile of driving, the object descended toward their car, which caused Barney to suddenly halt. It was large and quiet and occupied their entire field of view. He took hold of his binoculars and his loaded pistol, got out of the car, and steadily but slowly moved towards it. Through the binoculars, he could observe at least eight to eleven humanoid creatures. The object then began moving closer toward him and he got a better view of the creatures and claimed that they did not appear human. In hysteria, he sprinted back towards his vehicle and yelled to his wife that he thought that these humanoid creatures were out to capture them.

Barney drove as fast as he could, asking his wife to keep check of the other object. After a negligible period of time, they could hear a sequence of beeps and buzzes in sequence. This left them in a state of daze and altered their consciousness and state of mind. They heard the second set of beeps and buzzes which brought them back to their senses. They established that they had driven for 35 miles down the road, but had no recollection of it at all other than 3 very short instances in the whole journey.

The couple arrived back home at dawn. They tried to reconstruct the chronology of it all, but could not recollect most of it. Likewise, they did not remember some things like how their clothes got torn. Their watches also never worked again, and there were shiny circle patches on the bonnet of their car. These circles would alter the direction of a compass if it was brought close to them.

Betty's dress also had a pink powder all over it. She initially thought to throw it away fearing contamination and did, but she later recovered it in the hope of possibly finding answers from it.

The couple eventually got into contact with the Air Force and informed them of their encounter. However, they held back on some of the details with the fear that they would be judged as lunatics. Their case was eventually forwarded to Project Blue Book which was responsible for getting to the bottom of it. But by now, what lesson have we learned from our good friends down at Project Blue Book?

Betty nonetheless, decided that she wanted to investigate the matter on her own and borrowed a book on UFOs from the local library. She ended up writing to the author of the book, retired Marine Corp, Major Donald Keyhoe. Her letter eventually landed in the possession of an astronomer, Walter Webb since Betty had mentioned that the couple was considering hypnosis to try and reconstruct the whole event. Webb eventually met up with the couple and after about six hours of listening to their narrations and questions and answers, he believed that the Hills were telling the truth due to the consistency of their narrations. There were only a few uncertainties, but he ignored them and claimed that those were as a result of the human judgment.

The couple eventually had a hypnosis sessions. Barney would go first and then Betty, and they did this over a long time to try and establish what really happened. However, there were discrepancies in their recollections, for instance, Barney did not fully agree that they were abducted by the aliens and thought it was more of a coming together. The doctor, Benjamin Simon, noted that Barney's recollection might have been mixed up with the dreams that Betty had relayed to him and that Betty's account was the more accurate one. They all agreed though that the hypnosis session helped shed light on the issue. The hypnosis also relieved the Hill couple from the anxiety they had faced during the period after the ordeal.

The Hills were open to speaking about their interactions with the humanoid beings. They shared information freely and were not shy to speak on it. Through their collaboration together with Benjamin Simon, author John G Fuller published a famous and successful book that narrates the encounter with the extraterrestrials that the couple heard.

A story like this, of course, would have some strong refutations one would believe, and the rift was right down the middle. A good number of people did believe the couple, but similarly, a good number also did not.

There was the obvious fact that the Air Force report did not in any way correlate with that of the Hill couple. In fact, the Air

Force suggests that the only possible thing they could have seen was a weather balloon. It is also worth noting that Betty was a lifelong UFO fanatic, which then brings the credibility of the entire sighting into question. It is reported that Betty would occasionally spend hours, three to four times a week, staying awake in the hope of getting a glimpse of a UFO. Her fanaticism got to the point that she could not distinguish between a streetlight and a UFO, not to mention that she would also likewise claim that other objects were UFOs. There also is the bit that the hypnosis sessions took two years, which was more than enough for Betty and Barney to construct and master their story then narrate it perfectly during the sessions, even adding a few discrepancies to it simply to bring in that human judgment aspect into it.

However, the two main bits that totally disapprove the Hills' story is one, the blatant lack of evidence. Most other UFO sightings have had quite a number of people who can back up the account, for instance, the Washington Invasion, the Level land case, and Shag Harbor. The Hills' account was only between the couple and a third party, their dog. One would think that for such a vivid encounter, someone else would have noticed, even just one person. Second, researchers found out that the accounts given by the Hills had absurdly resounding similarities from fictional films, such as **Invaders from Mars** and **The Outer Limits.** At some point, it even felt like a mere reconstruction.

In conclusion, there is to date a lot of uncertainty on Unidentified Flying Objects let alone the existence of extraterrestrial life. This certainly means that, believer or not, we cannot and should not discredit any alleged sightings, encounters, or even abductions until they can be proven beyond reasonable doubt to being false, illegitimate and/or invalid. Nonetheless, it is safe to say that the Hills got this one horribly wrong. This was a simple case of fanaticism and delusion

Barney passed away aged 46 as a result of a brain hemorrhage on February the 25th, nine years later in 1969. Betty remained unmarried until her passing due to cancer on 17th October 2004.

CHAPTER SIX: LEVELLAND CASE, 1957

Levelland, a small town in Texas, experienced a UFO sighting that was viewed by a very large number of witnesses, which made it stunning and a rather bizarre encounter. Joel Salaz and Pedro Saucedo, two farm workers, were the first to report the sighting to the police. The latter spoke to Officer A.J. Fowler and narrated to him how they had seen a flashing light, blue in color as they drove 4 miles to the west of the small town. They asserted that as the rocket like object moved towards their truck, their engine died. In a panic, Saucedo claimed he jumped out of the truck. It then proceeded to fly directly above them with great speed. As it sped away, the truck's engine came back alive. The officer, however, disregarded the story as it did not sound believable. Little did he know that he was to receive a very similar call just an hour later. Another motorist, Jim Wheeler, reported to Officer Fowler that four miles east of Levelland on the road was an egg like shaped object that was very bright and obscured his path. His vehicle's engine, just like Salaz's and Saucedo's, had stopped. As he got out of his car to go investigate it, it took off and then his car's engine revved back up.

Reports came flooding in. First, it was a couple, who gave very similar accounts. Driving northeast of the tow, like the three previous witnesses, they saw an intensely bright flashing light that was moving in the sky and momentarily, for about 3 seconds, their radio and car headlights stopped working. More and more reports kept coming in from all over the town with very similar narrations.

By this time, the level of suspicion in the police department had grown and officers had begun investigating it. Two officers, Sheriff Weir Clem and Fire Chief Ray Jones also had similar encounters. There were a total of 15 reports in that short span and then they all stopped.

Like any other major UFO sighting, the Levelland case attracted a major media frenzy. Investigators from **Project Blue Book** (which we discuss in the Kenneth Arnold Incident) were sent to go analyze the case. However, the entire investigation was inadequately conducted, and it only took them seven hours to reach a conclusion. The investigators claimed that the intense rain and lighting that had been experienced in the area the past days had culminated in a **ball lightning** which caused the flashes of lightings, and the engine failure was as a result of "wet electrical circuits." Critics were quick to speak up.

James McDonald and J Allen, two prominent ufo-ologists quickly disagreed with the investigator's theories and provided their own findings.

CHAPTER SEVEN: BELGIAN WAVE, 1989-1990

Suitably, the sightings were called the Belgian Wave for a reason: They were a series of reported UFO sightings from November 29th,, 1989 all the way to the following year in April. The first account was witnessed by an estimated 30 different groups of people, including police officers. All the witnesses had similar stories, claiming that the object was flying very low and was very large. The supposed craft was triangular in shape, had lights beneath it, and was flat. It also made no sound as it moved above Belgium.

The Belgian Wave reached its climax last night of March in 1990. Objects that could not be identified were picked up on radar by the Belgian Air Force. The events were supposedly witnessed by about fourteen thousand people, a majority of whom reported the case. There were three peculiar lights which changed color. They were larger than stars and would either be red, yellow, or green. They seemed to lay in a formation of an equilateral triangle. The second set of lights, roughly ten minutes later appeared and moved towards the first. Eventually, a third also popped up. Two F-16 jets were deployed by the Air Force to go investigate, but every time they had a firm lock-on, the lights would toggle positions. They tried this for about half an hour, and the same thing would happen every time. After about forty minutes, they had their last loc-on, which was disrupted by a sudden acceleration from 160 kmph to 1120 kmph, which led to the loss of radar signal and was the last time they were observed.

Only a single photo of the whole encounter existed and was believed to be credible for the longest time possible, with the *Society of Belgian Studies of Natural Phenomena*

(SOBEPS) being the biggest supporter. However, the photographer, Patrick Marechal, spoke out and said that the photo was a hoax that he and his friends had created. They simply obtained a piece of Styrofoam, cut it into a triangular shape, and then proceeded to paint it black and rooted lights at each point. The final task was to suspend it by a string and attempt to take a believable picture. For twenty years, that photo was regarded as one solid piece of evidence for the Belgian Wave.

Over time, skeptics produced stellar evidence that the Belgian Wave was ill constructed by SOBEPS to get the Belgian people into believing in UFOs and subsequently extraterrestrial life. They also claimed that the lock-ons that the military jets obtained were in fact on each other. However, this does not entirely rule out that the Belgian Wave might actually have been an interstellar coming together of two species.

CHAPTER EIGHT: LONNIE ZAMORA, 1964

On Friday, April 24th, 1964, there was an alleged UFO sighting in the evening at about 10 minutes to six PM in the town of Socorro, New Mexico. There were a number of witnesses, but Lionne Zamora, a police officer, claimed to have had a close sighting and meeting with the supposed UFO, and this was the most detailed account made. But unlike almost every other UFO sighting, this one was different. There actually were bits of physical evidence left behind. If you remember, some notable sightings such as the Shag Harbour Incident had absolutely no evidence to support it and its witnesses. The Lonnie Zamora Incident left behind metal scrapings, a landing imprint on the ground, and burned vegetation.

Here's the account from Sergeant Zamora.

He was by himself in his patrol car and was pursuing a speeding vehicle that was headed south of the town of Socorro. At a quarter to six PM, he claimed to have a seen a flame and heard a thunderous sound emanate from the sky. He initially thought that dynamite had gone off. He called off the chase and went to investigate. He continued to head west and eventually could see an object that was shiny. According to Zamora, the object resembled a car that seemed to be overturned. He could make out two "people" standing next to it. One of the two people took off upon noticing him. He described the object as 'O' shaped and appeared aluminum. He goes on to state that he only caught a glimpse of the two people, but there was nothing odd about their appearance or stature.

He drove a few more feet and got out of his car and began walking towards the object. Having a better view, he says that the object was oval, appeared smooth, and he could not see any windows. After getting closer, there was a loud roar. He claimed that it began at a low frequency but loud, and its pitch rose. Frightened, he took off and ran. He ran while looking back at the object, bumped into his car, fell on the ground, and lost his spectacles. He got back up and ran a bit further fearing that it may harm him.

The object then began to rise, and at one point was level with his car. He claims that he saw it move in a straight line away from him maintaining its distance from the ground. It being a safe distance away, he ran back to his car and made a radio call to one of his colleagues and asked him to look out the window as the object was flying in his general direction. But his colleague, Nep Lopez, did not catch a glimpse of it and Sergeant Zamora recalls that this is because he did not specify which window.

He watched it get small and disappear in the distance.

A few moments later, he was joined by Sergeant Chavez, a colleague of his, whom he had given directions via the radio in his car, and they inspected the area. This was when they noticed the burning vegetation and soil and the landing marks that had been caused by the object. From the imprint on the ground, it appears that the object had four "legs."

Other corroborating witnesses also spoke up. A pair of tourists, driving through Socorro insisted that they saw an aircraft, which they believe resembled the shape of an egg, taking off with a trailing bluish flame.

Another tourist family assumed that the object that flew barely feet above their car was an airplane that was crash landing, since the airport in Socorro was not far from where they were. When they stopped for fuel, one of them jokingly said to the attendant that the airplanes in Socorro flew really low.

Following its widespread publish, and Air Force investigation was dispatched to try to get to the bottom of it. Quite suspiciously, the FBI requested that their presence remained anonymous. This led to Zamora making the assumption that the Air Force had been testing a new piece of equipment. However, they quickly shot down the notion. Measurements and samples were taken for analysis.

There has been a whole array of denial theories. Some state that local high school students had seemingly engineered it all as a prank to Zamora. Others claim ball lightning as in the Levelland case and some that it was merely a *dust devil*. One UFO skeptic even said that Zamora had seen a mirage.

The Air Force published an official report, but experts who went through it say it is riddled with unmissable errors. One example is their claim that there were no other witnesses and that there were no disturbances to the soil. Having still not solved it, the case is to this day open. Some people also questioned the Air Force's disregard of Zamora as those who met him praised him for being very credible and a serious police officer.

Even today, after years of investigation, and just like every other UFO related case that has passed through the hands of Project Blue Book, they hold that there is no substantial evidence to prove the notion that the incident was interstellar related, and despite them having not solved it yet, they hold that there is a sane, conventional explanation to it all.

As of today, the landing and take-off site still remains as it was in 1964 when the encounter happened.

Lonnie Zamora eventually got tired of the whole fiasco. He avoided people who tried to make contact with him on the subject and went on to work as a manager at a gas station. He died at age 76 of a heart attack in 2009.

CHAPTER NINE: WESTALL ENCOUNTER, 1966

April 6th, 1966 was the day that had more than 200 members and staff from two schools in Melbourne, Australia, lay claim to having witnessed what they held to be a UFO. At around eleven AM for nearly 20 minutes, they said an object came down on a nearby open field and later took flight towards the northwest. This is how the incident unfolded. It was late morning on a Wednesday and the students and teachers from Westall High school were just finishing up their sporting event. They then saw an object in the sky, which they estimated to be about twice the size of a family wagon, had an oval disk shape, and was gray with a hint of purple tone. The witnesses claimed that the oval object crossed the school and descended and disappeared behind a paddock of trees. After about 20 minutes, with witnesses obviously having increased as the news had begun to spread, the object ascended and at neck breaking speed, disappeared northwest of the school.

Believe it or not, the investigations into Westall 9166 have yielded nothing, absolutely nothing, not even an attempted explanation. Neither the witnesses (all two hundred of them) nor the teams responsible for investigating it have to this date come up with anything. Strange!

A reunion was held, in 2006, 40 years later that brought together the witnesses to commemorate the Westall sighting!

CHAPTER TEN: LUBBOCK LIGHTS, 1951

An unusual development of lights appeared and could be seen between August and September in 1951 in the city of Lubbock, Texas. They are regarded as one of the great UFO sightings of America, together with the like of Roswell and the Levelland Case. Initially, the military believed that the unusual lights were caused by plover birds; yes, you heard that right, birds! But they soon discarded that notion as not plausible. Well, obviously.

In their backyard sat three professors from Texas Technical University at about 2100 hours on August 25th, 1951. They claim to have witnessed about 20 to 30 flashes fly above them in a matter of seconds. They seemed as bright as stars, but larger in size. They at first did not think anything was unusual and thought they were simply meteors. However, they changed their minds once a second set flew above them. The three University dons then took to the local newspaper to give their accounts of the sighting. Once they had run the story, three women from the town came forward and stated that on the same night, they too had observed odd flashing lights. They were followed by another professor.

The first three professors to see the lights accompanied by two of their friends, two other professors, on September the 5th, were determined to have another sighting. They sat in the front yard and to their awe, the lights did fly above them. They were about fifteen this time and were about the size of a plate. They all felt a weird sensation when the lights passed above them.

It was night time on the last day of August, when a first year student from Texas Technical was lying in bed in his room, looking out of the window. He claimed to have seen a set of 18 to 20 lights that seemed to gather above and fly over his house. They appeared to make a V sort of formation. He went into the house and took his camera, a 35mm Kodak, and then strolled out onto the terrace of his home to check whether he would be able to spot the lights again. Eventually, he did as two more sets flew above him, and he managed to take a total of five photos, soon after which the lights disappeared. In the wake of having the photographs created, Hart then went into Lubbock's local magazine, The Avalanche, with the photos. After inspecting the photographs Jay Harris, the paper's editor, told Hart that he would print his photos in the following day's paper, but in the event that the photos were a sham, Hart would be in big trouble. At the point, Hart guaranteed that the photographs were bona fide. Harris gave compensation of ten dollars to Hart in exchange for them. The photos were soon reproduced in daily papers all over the country and featured in Life magazine, giving them wide attention.

It has never been proven that Hart's photos were fake, but neither can anyone validate that they are genuine. The professors, however, claimed that the lights they saw flew in a 'U' formation as opposed to Hart's, which were in a 'V.'

Towards the end of September the same year, Lieutenant Rupplet read about these strange occurrences and chose to investigate them. He found his way to the city of Lubbock and questioned witnesses, including the professors. It was then that Rupplet inferred that what they had seen must have been plover birds. The birds, it is believed, were flying over the city for their annual migration. What caused the lights though? It was thought that the lights were a mere reflection of streetlights off the birds' undersides. A local farmer agreed with the Lieutenant as he personally clearly saw the birds and could distinctly make out that they were in fact plovers. Another farmer and his wife were also puzzled by the flying lights. They saw a second set, and to their disbelief, a third began to circle their house. After a short time, however, they could make out bird sounds. This theory was supported by Project Blue Book: yes, the very same one.

Another thing disapproved the plover theory: The head photographer of the local newspaper in Lubbock took some photos of migrating plovers and compared them with the ones Hart took, and they were distinctively different. This ruled out the possibility that it could have been birds. Similarly, as per a game warden that was also interviewed by the Lieutenant, the lights simply couldn't have been a result of plover birds for two reasons. One, plovers fly at a speed of about 50 mph, which was much slower than what witnesses had estimated the lights to be moving at. Two, plovers flew in much smaller flocks, and most people stated that the lights were up to twenty. However, he did not rule out the possibility of large flocks though they are rare. The one last thing that also made it evident that these could not have been birds was the size, the lights were much larger than any plover. The Lieutenant himself eventually wrote a book about the entire investigation. He admitted in the book that the lights could not and were not a result of migrating plover birds, but plainly refused to state or explain what caused the lights.

During his investigation, witnesses also claimed to have seen a flying wing. It was enormous and made no sound, which are two common witness accounts in almost all UFO sightings. The Lieutenant was aware that the Air Force did possess a bomber jet referred to as the 'flying wing', but could not decipher why witnesses claimed it was soundless because the bomber could be heard.

Later it was established that the Lubbock Lights were neither alien crafts nor plover birds and were simple naturally occurring phenomena. However, these claims did not have much weight to them as with numerous investigations by either the project Blue Book or the Air Force. This is because they did not explain their findings nor did they reveal the identity of the scientists involved in the findings and all in anonymity sake. This does not, however, mean that their findings are true nor are they false.

CHAPTER ELEVEN: PHOENIX LIGHTS

Phoenix, Arizona and Sonora, Mexico were the locations of UFO sightings in the form of lights in 1997, on Thursday, March the 13th. Multiple reports with different descriptions were issued on that night by literally thousands of people from around half past seven PM through three hours till half past ten PM. The reports came from about three hundred miles apart from Nevada, through Phoenix, all the way to Tucson.

That night, witnesses gave two accounts of different sightings. One was of a set of mobile lights that flew over Arizona in what was described as a triangular sort of layout (very similar to what was witnessed in Belgium during their wave of sightings), and a second set were static lights seen over Phoenix. The latter was identified, however, by the Air Force to have been flares that were dropped during a training session by one of their aircraft.

The initial sighting left an eerie impact on its witnesses. They gave an account of seeing an enormous craft, a couple of football fields large. It was shaped like a V and hovered lucidly over the Phoenix skies. Like all other sightings, it made no sound at all. It had five visible lights. The governor was also one of the witnesses who attested to the sighting, however, at the time, he denied the notion of a possible alien aircraft. Nonetheless, years later, he did admit that what he saw could not have been from this world.

The first sighting of this unidentified flying object was in Henderson, Nevada. A man reported he had to see what seemed like a Boeing 747, but was not and sounded like fast-moving wind. He claimed it had six lights. The second report came in from a retired police officer driving in Paulden, Arizona. He could make out red and orange lights in the sky.

He returned home and watched the lights through a pair of binoculars until they faded away and disappeared. These two were just the first two reports.

Calls began straggling in from all over Prescott Valley. People claimed to have seen an object in the sky with a distinct cluster of lights. The object, V shaped, had five reddish lights and one notably white one on its tip. The lights were arranged along its edges in a triangular formation. This account was very similar amongst all the people that called in to report the odd sighting in the town of Prescott. The object, which hovered around for about two to three minutes, then flew directly above those that were gathered to get a look at it and turned sharply to the right and disappeared. They inferred that the object was indeed solid in nature as it blocked out the stars as it passed by on a clear night.

The same shape and formation were then reported ten miles from the town of Prescott in Dewey by at least six people who were all driving along the same highway.

The first sighting in Phoenix was of a family of five. They could first make out the lights from very far out, about 100 km. After ten minutes of trying to figure out what exactly they were looking at, the lights grew visibly larger, and they could make out the exact same characteristics as had been described by every other witness thus far. As it got closer to them, they realized that it was headed in their direction. They thought that it looked like a sixty-degree carpenter square. At one moment, the object was just about 100 feet directly above them. It continued to move overhead and vanished deeper into the ranges of the mountains.

The first sighting in Phoenix was by a cement driver who was a staunch UFO denier and skeptic. However, driving down a hill, he observed the unidentified object with its lights, hovering soundlessly through the night sky and was left astounded and in awe. He admitted that for all his denying, what he saw did not have any conventional explanation and he was inclined to believing that he had seen a UFO and started to admit the possibility of extraterrestrial life. A pilot manning a small plane had also seen the strange alignment of lights, but after referring them to air traffic control, they relayed that nothing unusual appeared on their radars. The same formation was later reported past Phoenix in Kingman. The man pulled over to the side of the road and reported the incident to the police using a nearby pay phone.

There were stints in 2007 and 2008 were similar formations re-appeared. There also are photographs and videos from the initial happenings that exist today and can be found on the internet.

Since there were two separate sets of lights, two possible explanations had to be proposed. As for the second account, it was clearly established to have been flares. Pilot Lieutenant Colonel Ed Jones confirmed that on that night he flew an A-10 Warthog together with four others and dropped burning flares around the area. This is confirmed by the analysis of the wind data on that day, which changed course to some of the areas where the sightings occurred. Also, unlike many UFO sighting, the Phoenix case had one particularly notable omission, speed. The witnesses did not claim that the lights moved at blistering speeds as in other accounts, such as the Kenneth Arnold Case, the Levelland case, or even the Washington Airport Invasion and almost every other sighting. Witnesses claimed that the lights hovered above them, which simply means that the lights could simply be blown by the wind and such are the case with the flares.

As for the first sighting, which was an extensive series of people seeing a V shaped object in the sky, there still is no concrete explanation for it. However, many researchers have reached a general consensus that those were actually planes. A phenomenon, called the *illusory contour,* could cause people to see single lines, or dots moving in unison and a single object or shape. It is believed that that individual planes flying over the area could have been confused or thought to be a single flying object. Upon careful analysis of some of the video tapes, it was discovered that the lights were moving individually and not as a group. It is almost believed that the formation might have been caused by the military jets during their training sessions since they fly in similar formations! However, witnesses and believers heckled the explanation and did not find it in any way befitting of what they had witnessed.

CHAPTER TWELVE: THE RENDLESHAM FOREST INCIDENT, 1980

Rendlesham Forest was perhaps Britain's most infamous UFO sighting. It is usually referred to as the Roswell of Britain. In 1980, towards the end of December, strange, unexplained, and unidentified lights could be seen near the forest of Rendlesham. The reports were later tied to claims that a UFO landing actually took place in the forest. The United States Air Force had a base at RAF Woodbridge very close to the forest, and Lieutenant Colonel Charles Halt was among those who attested to seeing the apparent UFO.

At 3 AM on Boxing Day, 1980, lights were seen going down into the forest from the RAF Woodbridge by a patrol brigade. They at first, reasoned that it could be a downed aircraft and went into the forest to investigate. Upon close encounter, they found a metallic object that was glowing and emitting different colored lights. They attempted to get closer and get a better view, but the object moved away from them into the trees. It is reported that there was unrest with the animals in nearby farms during the time of the encounter (however, that cannot be termed as viable evidence for a UFO sighting as animals have been known to go into frenzies even during natural phenomena like earthquakes and storms). One serviceman even went on ahead to state that what he had witnessed was certainly a craft of unknown origin. However, no one has stepped up to support his account nor have there been any corroborations.

About an hour later, at four AM, police were called to come and take a look, but from their reports, only light from a nearby lighthouse was visible at the time. Once it was morning, and with the help of daylight, the servicemen that had first gone to inspect the sight went back in. They found tiny triangular imprints on the ground. There were also a number of broken branches and some burned vegetation. The police were summoned again to come take a look, but all they could agree on was that the triangular imprints could only have been caused by an animal.

The deputy base commander, who was one of those who saw the first light, and Lt. Col. Halt went to the supposed site two days later. Their main aim was to acquire radiation samples from the area. However, they conflicted on how important the readings they got were and even whether they actually made a difference. During Halt's investigation, another flashing light was seen to the east of their location. However, the lighthouse was in a similar direction, and it is thought that the light came from it. Lt. Col. Halt went on to write a memo about the encounter which was later made public. In the memo, Halt blamed both the US and UK government for conspiracy and covering up the exact happenings.

 A number of witnesses were interviewed regarding the lights, and while all of them admitted to seeing the light, they did admit that they did not find anything unusual and they all thought that the light came from the lighthouse that was nearby. One person also noticed the animal unrest similar to Halt.

Thirty years later, Halt agreed to go on record again and retell his story, where he reiterated that the event was caused by extraterrestrials and the two governments had linked up and conspired to keep it under wraps. However, the base commander came out and claimed that they did not find anything that was close Halt's encounter and that they had people to prove that nothing unusual was found in Rendlesham Forest. The police who had also been called two times to investigate the scene, sided with the base commander adding that Halt's account was untrue. They believed that everything about the alleged encounter was ordinary and perfectly explainable. The light was from the lighthouse and the imprints from animals in the forest.

However, when the Ministry of Defense released their files in 2001, something stood out. The depth, or lack thereof, of the entire investigation was rather bewildering. The investigative party simply blew off the incident as if the claims did not carry any weight at all. Their explanation is that the incident did not seem to have the potential to threaten national security. Therefore, they did not feel the need to investigate it as an issue regarding security. People began to speculate that this was a ploy by the two governments to keep extraterrestrial life a secret to the public. This is how this incident was likened to Roswell.

However, sadly, this was also another classic case of misinterpretation. Skeptics believed that no such UFO encounter had happened due to the clear lack of evidence and the fact that the lights could have easily come from the nearby lighthouse. Scientists then claimed that the light could have either come from the lighthouse or was naturally occurring nocturnal lights.

CHAPTER THIRTEEN: THE CARSON SINK INCIDENT, 1952

The 24th of July, 1952 saw two pilots flying over Carson Sink to the west of Nevada at around twenty minutes to 4 PM encounter an unidentified flying object.

The occurrence was reported by two veteran pilots and military professionals, Lt. Col. John L McGinn and Lt. Col. John R Barton. They were on a strict Pentagon assignment at the time he spotted the claimed UFO. Having a very good knowledge of aircraft, they could not have confused it with anything else.

The two men were north of San Francisco at Hamilton Field. They demanded a double motor B-25 plane to use while on their assignment. They set out towards Colorado with perfect flying conditions. Between Sacramento, California, and Reno, Nevada, the pilots entered the Green 3 flying roadway to Salt Lake City, Utah. At about eleven thousand feet, while flying over Carson Sink, twenty minutes to four PM, they saw what they thought were 3 airplanes in front of them and on their right side. Initially, they expected that the obscure airplanes were F-86 contenders, in view of their developments, however, they understood that the airships were highly noticeable. In addition, the airships were flying in an immaculate V development, which was exceptionally irregular for military planes.

They steered their jet towards the flying object, but upon a better look, they were in awe. They saw that the airships were a splendid silver color with a Delta-wing airfoil. However, they did not have any tails or flight shelters, which each known airship had.

Neither of the two men had ever seen anything even slightly close to the airships. As they continued observing the three objects in questions, they stepped to the left and flew rapidly to within 400 - 800 yards of their jet, which was an awkwardly short amount of space. The two men assessed the speed of the obscure flying machine to be no less than 3 times that of any aircraft either of them knew. In about four very rapid seconds, the object flew past them and disappeared from their sight.

When McGinn and Barton arrived at the headquarters of the Air Defense Command in Colorado Springs, they discovered that no nonmilitary personnel or military flying machine was anywhere close to the Carson Sink at the time of their encounter. Specifically, all known delta-wing planes, at that point flown only by the Navy, were nowhere near the region for that matter. The closest thing to the Delta Wing, which was navy blue in color, was in fact miles away at that particular time on the West Coast.

McGinn and Barton vehemently refuted the notion that what they came across was F-86 planes, since the two makes resembled each other and could easily be confused for one another. Air Defense Command transferred the answer to Project Blue Book. An examination was begun at once, yet the episode was formally left as unexplained.

CHAPTER FOURTEEN: THE YENI KENT COMPOUND, 2008

A compound in Kumburgaz/Istanbul was the venue for what we can regard to as a paranormal event and nothing short of that. The sightings were viewed by numerous inhabitants and recorded by Yalcin Yalman, a night security guard from 2007 to 2009. No previous pictures or recordings have proven as important for the study and understanding of extraterrestrial visits. They have been constantly called upon where digital evidence of extraterrestrial life is requiring and are deemed very credible.

Amid the long stretches of April and May 2009, Turkey saw a nationwide surge of UFO reports, cases, sightings, and incidents in multiple cities, some of which were actually photographed and aired. Inside a similar timeframe, night guard Mr. Yalcin Yalman, a resident and occupant of Kumburgaz working at Yeni Kent compound, caught sightings of these bizarre and unidentified objects and recorded them several times. The recordings have gone an amazingly long way in studying unidentified flying objects and are considered pretty much the closest thing to actual evidence for UFOs and extraterrestrial life. In these astonishing UFO video recordings which have real repercussions around the globe and are recorded as "the most critical UFO recordings ever," physical types of UFO's and their metallic structures are plainly discernible. What's more essential is that in the recordings of the supposed alien crafts, elements in them can be unmistakably made out. It should be mentioned that the pictures and recordings by the night guard, Mr. Yalman, are a hundred percent authentic. They have been subjected to numerous tests by different organizations, and they have come to the conclusion that they were not fabricated and can be used as a credible source since their validity had already been put to question a number of times over. Some of the findings include that the actual date of the recordings was factual, the recordings were taken by the said camera, and the moving objects in the crafts were real and not computer CGIs.

It is also believed that these objects were physical and tangible in nature and their structures were of a material that isn't known to us, for example, climate inflatables and so fall into the classification UFO's.

The Yeni Kent compound remains to be one of the most vivid UFO sightings yet. Regardless of the fact that the sightings have not been explained yet, it is by far the most believable of them all. However, it is agreed upon that the object in the pictures and recording are unidentified flying objects, this does not tie them to extraterrestrial life. More often than not, these complex cases have very simple explanations.

CHAPTER FIFTEEN: TEHRAN UFO INCIDENT, 1976

The morning of September 19[th,] 1976 saw two F-4 phantom jets that were flying over the Capital of Iran, Tehran, come into contact with an Unidentified Flying Object. The pilots reported that the instruments aboard their jets failed as they approached it, but soon resumed functioning once they withdrew. One of the jets tried to fire a missile at the foreign object, but the pilot soon realized that that was not working too.

However, studies soon found out that there were very simple explanations to all of these accounts. One, it is believed by a number of investigators that the objects that the two pilots saw were likely the planet Jupiter. Due to very rare encounters, people are likely to misidentify it, and also pilot incompetence was blamed. As for equipment failure, this particular jet, the F-4 Phantom was notorious for electrical short circuits and malfunctions!

CHAPTER SIXTEEN: BERWYN MOUNTAINS CRASH

In the year 1974 on the 23rd of January, individuals announced hearing a colossal blast, experienced the ground shaking, and bore witness to a splendid light. This light emanated from the horizon of the nearby Berwyn Mountains. The households in the towns of Llandrillo and Llandderfel were concluding their day and relaxing in front of the TV when a blast was heard that caused the earth to shake up to a 3.5 on the Richter scale. Pandemonium followed as everybody ran from within their houses in fear that yet another tremor would be imminent. As they stood outside they saw an explosion of very bright light coming from the mountainside.

Police centered in on the zone, and crisis administrations were placed on standby. In spite of the fact that pursuits were attempted, authoritatively nothing was found – prompting accusations of concealment.

STORIES

Forty years following that event, there has been numerous discussions and debates trying to unravel the true happenings of that night. Similarly, a lot of books have been written and films made with regards to the same.

A few specialists have guaranteed a UFO crashed, and additionally states "bodies" were recovered and taken away by officers. Different hypotheses have suggested it was a meteor that caused a quake whose epicenter was thought to be Bala Lake and the misperception that the lights were from a group of poachers.

Throughout the years, a lot more data has been brought to our attention but provided no solution, only questions. In 2008, the Daily Post procured official records indicating how Gwynedd Police were barraged with calls and observer records of the peculiar occasion, with some persuaded they had spotted a UFO. They gave an interesting understanding into what was happening that night.

A witness who saw the event on the slope said in an announcement: "[I] saw brilliant red light, similar to coal fire red. Vast immaculate circle. Like a major campfire witnessed lights above and on one side and the white lights advancing towards the base. The light changed shading between yellowish stained white and back."

A message detailed in a log by the police stated: "There's been an expansive blast in the range and from it a huge fire in the mountainside. From where I was, I could see it."

A wire message to boss constable Gwynedd, at eleven PM on the twenty-third of January stated: Saw brilliant green lights, question with tail – voyaging west. Saw about Bangor bearing – dropped down."

At approx. ten PM on the twenty-third of January: "Saw a roundabout light above a what could be a statue of one thousand five hundred feet. This question detonated and pieces tumbled to the ground. Mr ...... gauges the pieces probably would have dropped into the ocean amongst Rhyl and Liverpool."

In the year 2010, a key witness, Pat Evans, insisted she saw something from the mountainside. At the time she stated: "It (the protest) couldn't have there some other route separated from being flown there, so it must be a UFO or something to that effect. I'm looking at something that could just have there by flying and landing."

Ms. Evans, who was living in Llandderfel, close Bala, included: "We just observed this enormous ball sparkling and throbbing on the mountain. A few lights appeared to be scattered around it, and I simply wish we'd remained to perceive what the final product was – whether it would simply vanish or take off.

"We didn't see anyone out and about despite the fact that there were different reports that we were advised to leave by equipped police and military and so forth, which was all absolutely false.

"We'd heard a god-like blast, and we inhabit the foot of the mountain. It was my presumption that it might have been a plane crash. As a medical attendant and my young ladies being members of the St John (Ambulance), I figured that we could have been of some assistance."

No more official data was available regarding that particular event. A representative from the Research Department of the RAF Museum proposed photoflash procedures were utilized for preparing activities to enlighten the ground underneath.

CHAPTER SEVENTEEN: CLYDE W TOMBAUGH SIGHTING, 1949

Clyde William Tombaugh is a famed American astronomer who is credited with the discovery of Pluto in 1930. This was the first object in the Kuiper belt to be discovered. Pluto was at first regarded a planet, but its status later changed to a dwarf planet seventy-six years later in 2006. He was a serious researcher on UFOs and did manage to spot some. He was also a believer in existence of extraterrestrial life.

On August 20, 1949, close to Las Cruces, New Mexico, the astronomer saw what he thought were UFOs. They were six to eight lights in a rectangular formation, and he questioned whether the reflection he was seeing was something earthly because never occurred again. He was caught so off guard by such a peculiar sight and he was both frightened and in awe.

CHAPTER EIGHTEEN: MASS SIGHTINGS OF UFOs

As previously noted in the chapter above, a good number of the UFO accounts recorded had simply one or two witnesses, apart from Westall in Australia, which had well over 200 witnesses, with most of them either being pilots or motorists. Also, very few of these accounts happen in broad daylight, besides some cases like the Lonnie Zamora sighting. Some UFO sightings, however, seem to break all the rules and 'expose' themselves to large audiences at one time. Here is a look at some unidentified objects that were viewed by the masses. It is safe to mention though that most of these are usually quite simply explainable and cause no alarm.

June 1st, Tennessee: It was early morning in Burritt College and the sun was just beginning to rise, various understudies—who clearly were ambitious people back then, as well—were startled to see two brilliant questions in the sky. One of their teachers, who had explained the encounter in a letter said that the initial one resembled a little new moon, while the other looked like a substantial star. The little question at that point disappeared, whereas the greater one changed its form; initially a sphere or globe and then went flat into an extension that lay parallel to the sky. The little flash at that point appeared unmistakably once more, and expanded quickly as the other object visible became smaller. The both kept changing in a comparable manner for the following half an hour. "The understudies have requested a clarification, yet neither the President nor Professors are fulfilled with regards to the character of the lights," composed Carnes. While he himself estimated that the event might have been caused some way or another by barometrical dampness, the episode remains a puzzle.

The aircraft supposedly broke and slowed down and collided with a windmill found on the property belonging to a neighborhood judge, dissipating flotsam and jetsam onto more than a few sections of land. "The pilot of the ship should have been the just a single on board and, while his remaining parts were gravely, sufficiently deformed of the first has been gotten to demonstrate that he was not a tenant of this world," as indicated by the Morning News. Doubters have for a very long time rejected the record as a trick. In any case, for the year 1973, a journalist from the United Press found a 91-year-old occupant, Mary Evans, a lady who recalled her folks going by the site of the crash, and disclosing to her that the UFO pilot's body had been buried in the town's burial ground.

February 25, 1942: The Battle of Los Angeles: In the early morning hours, radar administrators detected an unknown blimp about a hundred and twenty miles in the west of the city Angels and observed restlessly as it hovered to within a couple of miles of the drift of southern California and after that mysteriously disappeared from their screens. At some point after that, a mounted guns officer along the drift announced what he witnessed 25 airships flying at an estimated distance of 25,000 feet, and a few minutes after the fact, different onlookers saw an inflatable like object conveying what seemed, by all accounts, to be flames over adjacent Santa Monica. At that point, witnesses spotted what they later liked to swarms of objects flying at different elevations, at speeds reaching 200 miles for each hour. Expecting that their beloved city was facing assault by the Japanese, they let go almost 1500 rounds of ammo at the intruder. In any case, clearly, none of them struck their target, in light of the fact that no downed craft was found. Authorities at first credited the occurrence to a mix of a false caution and mass insanity. However, UFO-ologists have hypothesized throughout the years that the heavy armament specialists may have been shooting at an extraterrestrial shuttle.

January 7, 1948: Saucer Appears Over Kentucky: Early in the evening, many inhabitants from Madisonville, KY region called the police to report that they witnessed what the account later described as "a roundabout object drifting overhead and emitting a splendid gleam." Police at that point cautioned Air Force authorities at the air base at Fort Knox. After 15 minutes, the landing strip's tower team detected the UFO also and utilized the radio to solicit a squadron from P-51 contenders to examine. Squadron pioneer Capt. Thomas Mantell, Jr., a specialist pilot, recounted that he did recognize the UFO and was interested. "I'm shutting in now to investigate," Mantell detailed in what would be his last radio call at a quarter past three PM. "The thing looks metallic, and is huge in the measure." After about three minutes, the pilot crashed and was killed. The official conclusion was that he had come up short on oxygen, yet UFO-ologists have since questioned that clarification.

Dec. 9, 1965: The Kecksburg Incident: Kecksburg, a small town in Pennsylvania around forty miles from Pittsburgh, was witness to what they termed as a green flame streaking across the sky before it crashed in a field. This occurred before dusk at six p.m. that night. Nearby occupant Bill Bulebush, who was taking a shot with his auto when he saw the object in question, described it as shaped like an oak seed and about double the length of a

Volkswagen Beetle. He said that it skimmed before making a U-turn and going down. A neighborhood fire fighter, James Romansky, later described the brought down aircraft as having hieroglyphic-like writing around its base ring. He just got the opportunity to inspect the aircraft for around quarter an hour before authorities from the military and the government arrived and requested everybody to evacuate the scene and erected barriers around the border. In this manner, there was the hypothesis that the object might have been a Soviet satellite, yet UFO specialist Clifford Stone, who talked years after the fact to previous Soviet authorities, said they insisted that the object had not been from any of theirs. After investigative writer, Leslie Keen, recorded a Freedom of information Act suit, NASA in the year 2009, any documentation on this topic was absent.

March 24, 1983: Hudson Valley: The rural range, around an hour outside of New York City to the north, bore witness to more than 5,000 UFO sightings from the year 1982 all the way through to 1986; maybe one of the greatest groups of occurrences ever. One night, on March 24, stands out due to the utter bulk—over 300 occupants called a neighborhood UFO Association's hotline that night, revealing that they had witnessed expansive angular exhibit of lights that moved gradually and quietly through the sky. A few witnesses drew sufficiently near to state that the aircraft was large enough to be a "flying city." Hunt Middleton, a neighborhood inhabitant who had quite recently arrived from New York City at half past seven p.m., described a line of six or seven amazingly brilliant lights. "They were all squinting on and off and were red, blue, green, and white. I knew it was no kind of customary airship on the grounds that the lights were stationary. It was simply floating there in the sky." Middleton claimed that he watched the object in question for about five minutes before going inside his home to get his family to come out and see it. At that point, it had disappeared.

March 13, 1997: The Phoenix Lights: On that night, a huge number of individuals in Nevada and the neighboring state of Arizona purportedly observed what people described as a monstrous, V-shaped object sketched out by what they counted to be seven lights. Others, notwithstanding, revealed observing spheres as well as triangles in the sky too. Police officers in the respective urban areas were stuck with reports from inhabitants. One man, Dana Valentines, a witness said that he and his dad both watched as these lights hovered 500 feet straightforwardly over them. "We could see the blueprint of a mass behind the lights, yet you couldn't really observe the mass," he says. "It was more similar to a dark bending of the night sky, wavy. I don't know precisely what it was, yet I know it's not an innovation general society has known recently." The military later asserted that National Guard pilots had discharged diversionary flares while on a preparation run, yet not every person acknowledged that clarification.

July 14, 2001: New Jersey Turnpike: Rural New Jersey, very close the city of New York was witness to bizarre yellow lights from the early morning of July 14th well into the early morning of the following day in 2001, and witnesses included a cop who watched in surprise. Later that night, at around half past midnight, another witness, Carteret Lt. Dan Tarrant, supposedly received a call while at home from his 19-year-old daughter, who was out with companions and had seen interesting lights. Tarrant told the Record and ABC News that he at that point ventured outside to investigate. As Tarrant revealed to ABC, what he had just observed was dumbfounding: "16 brilliant orange shaded lights, a few out of a V-sort arrangement. Others were dispersed surrounding the V." Tarrant relayed to the Record, a neighborhood daily paper, that the puzzling lights flashed over the sky for around 10 minutes and at that point blurred one after the other into haziness.

January 8, 2008: The Stephenville Lights: At night, almost forty neighborhood inhabitants, including a beginner pilot and a cop, saw an object that floated just above the cultivating group for around five minutes before streaking ceaselessly into the sky. Cop L.R. Gaitan disclosed to a radio station that he had been strolling to his car when he saw an iridescent object that brought back pictures of ejecting springs of gushing lava, suspended three thousand feet noticeable all around

CHAPTER NINETEEN: OTHER SIGNIFICANT UFO SIGHTINGS ACROSS THE GLOBE

One would agree that our list is predominantly American other than one or two sightings, for example, Shag Harbor, which is perhaps one of the strangest ones on the list. This, however, might be due to the simple reason that at the times of these encounters, most of the world had not yet been introduced to the possibility of extraterrestrial and alien life just like early in the day when people simply associated anything in the sky that they could identify as a simple religious intervention. Also, lack of reports from other parts of the world could be a result of the lack of means of documentation. We also saw some cases in the United States that took a while to catch on simply because there were no telephones back then and the fastest means of communication was not fast at all. Case in point was the infamous Roswell, where foreman Brasel heard of the UFO crash two weeks after he had already collected suspected debris from the crash site. The two combined factors might be the reason reports from other regions of the world are not as many, nonetheless, here are some cases that featured elsewhere.

McMinnville Episode, Oregon, Canada (1950): Evelyn Trent initially recognized a shimmering, metal-like plate early in the night sky as she was outside feeding her rabbits. Her agriculturist spouse looked for two or three minutes and after that chose to take two photographs before the unknown object disappeared. The couple avoided any exposure and declined to reveal the photos to the media, liking to keep the news to themselves to abstain from getting into an issue with the administration. Just a single neighborhood journalist lucked out. While endeavors have been made to look at the photos for any deceit, none has been successful at that to this given day. Until their passing in the nineties, the couple genuinely demanded that the photographs were of a real UFO.

Manbhum, Bihar, India (1957): At minimum 800 people of the villages of Kadori, Borsa, and Mangalda left their cottages to catch a glimpse of an extremely weird event. An unidentified flying object slipped to a height of 500ft over the ground, buzzing like a vehicle's motor. It drifted in the air for a few minutes and shot away at a mind boggling speed, leaving behind a great deal of smoke.

The Canary Islands sightings, Spain (1976): Residents of the Gran Canaria detailed observing a tremendous, lustrous blue circle floating above the ground. They claimed to have seen two figures in the monstrous circle, measuring 30m in breadth. The figures appeared to be shaped like humanoids. The circle became bigger and bigger before at last vanishing. At half past nine PM on that night, the Navy workforce witnessed a peculiar light travelling along the skyline that later dispersed into two particular items.

Iranian UFO pursuit (1976): The morning of September 19[th,] 1976 saw two F-4 phantom jets flying over the Capital of Iran, Tehran, come into contact with an Unidentified Flying Object. The pilot reported that the instruments aboard their jets failed as they approached it but soon resumed functioning once they withdrew. One of the jets tried to fire a missile at the foreign object, but the pilot soon realized that that was not working too.

However, studies sooner found out that there were very simple explanations to all of these accounts. One, it is believed by a number of investigators that the objects that the two pilots saw were likely the planet Jupiter. Due to very rare encounters, people are likely to misidentify it and also pilot incompetence was blamed. As for equipment failure, this particular jet, the F-4 Phantom was notorious for electrical short circuits and malfunctions.

Hudson Valley, New York sightings (1981): This sighting is particularly interesting because just like the Westall sighting, it had numerous reports, but unlike most other sightings, the flying object was similar to those from the Belgian wave and appeared triangular. The shocking and alarming bit as reported was, for their sheer size (some even claiming that they resembled a floating city) the objects did not make a sound as they hovered above Hudson Valley.

Japan Air Lines Flight 1628 (1986): The team of the flight making its way from Paris to Tokyo was joined by what they claimed were multiple UFOs for around an hour as the Boeing 747 payload transporter traveled over Alaska. The UFOs made movements that suggested gravity had no impact on them at all. Air movement controllers were not ready to recognize any UFO action around the Boeing notwithstanding rehashed affirmations by the team. The pilot, Captain Kenju Terauchi, is as solid a source as one could discover as he had filled in as a military pilot and logged over 10,000 hours in flight.

Kolkata, India (2007): An intense fireball, almost something from a sci-fi movie, threatened and scared the residents of Kokota in 2007. Half an hour to four AM in the morning, October the 29th, they, the residents and witnesses, described the immense object as a moving, vanishing wad of flame across the sky. Researchers endeavored to stick a characteristic vast marvel tag on it, in any case, stating that the shape-moving capacity made it difficult to distinguish its birthplaces.

CONCLUSION

As we conclude, we first and foremost hope that this has been an enlightening journey and you have certainly learned a lot. The issue of Unidentified Flying Objects is a deep one and needs an in depth and analytical approach. Throughout the chapters, we have seen and learned of encounters from across the globe. This certainly means that UFOs are not the creation of two people inside a basement somewhere, and are rather a global phenomenon.

We are also left with a number of questions. The biggest of them all is whether there is a conspiracy by top governments to keep the discovery of some of these UFOs a secret as seen in famous cases such as Roswell and the Rendlesham Forest lights. If the answer to the above question is yes, then it creates a domino effect of more questions, the main one being whether these top governments have kept the existence of alien life a secret from the public. This would definitely change the scope of a lot of things, knowing that we are not the only species. What could we learn from this foreign species? Where are they from? What do they want? Do they bring harm? But as the public, we hope that if the answer was yes, that they have preserved this secret for the greater good.

Let's also look at it from a different perspective and stop blaming our governments for everything for once. We have seen so many cases in this book of sightings being hoaxes or simple delusions. What if extraterrestrial life is a simple creation of the human mind?

As the famous saying goes, all we have to do is wait and find out.

FREE BOOKS

Sign up to my newsletter for free Kindle books.

By joining my newsletter you will be notified when my books are free on Amazon so you can download them and not have to pay!

You will also be notified when I release a new book and be able to buy it for a reduced price.

You will also get a free **Spartans and the Battle of Thermopylae** book delivered to your inbox (in **PDF** format) that can be read on your laptop, phone, or tablet.

Finally you will also receive free history articles delivered to your inbox once a week.

Simply click the link below to signup and receive your free book:
https://nostramo.lpages.co/tom-king/

Made in the USA
Columbia, SC
13 December 2018